W9-DHR-848

STRESSED
OUT
STUDENTS
GUIDE
TO
SAYING
NO
TO
CHEATING

STRESSED OUT STUDENTS GUIDE TO SAYING NO TO CHEATING

Series Editor
Lisa Medoff, Ph.D.

KAPLAN PUBLISHING

© 2008 Kaplan, Inc.

Published by Kaplan Publishing, a division of Kaplan, Inc.
1 Liberty Plaza, 24th Floor
New York, NY 10006

Printed in the United States of America

First printing: 2008
10 9 8 7 6 5 4 3 2 1

SOS: Stressed Out Students' Guide to Saying No to Cheating
ISBN-13: 978-1-4277-9806-0

Kaplan Publishing books are available at special quantity discounts to use for sales promotions, employee premiums, or educational purposes. Please email our Special Sales Department to order or for more information at kaplanpublishing@kaplan.com, or write to Kaplan Publishing, 1 Liberty Plaza, 24th Floor, New York, NY 10006.

Got stress?

Learn how to confront and resist the
temptations that lead to academic
shortcuts.

Stories and real-life advice told *by*
teens *for* teens to help cope with
stress—for students and parents alike.

ABOUT THE SERIES EDITOR

Lisa Medoff holds a B.A in psychology from Rice University, an M.S.Ed. in school counseling from the University of Pennsylvania, and a Ph.D. in child and adolescent development from Stanford University.

For the past ten years, Lisa has been working with middle and high school students who have learning disabilities and emotional disorders. In this job, Lisa consults with both families and schools to help them provide the optimal school and home environments for their children with special needs.

She has taught child & adolescent development and psychology courses to both undergraduates and teacher credential candidates at Stanford University, Santa Clara University and San Jose State University.

Lisa works with the non-profit Cleo Eulau Center of Palo Alto, providing consulting services and teacher education workshops for elementary school teachers in a high-risk school district. She is also the author of a weekly child psychology column for the website Education.com.

CONTENTS

CONTENTS

CONTENTS

CONTENTS

CONTENTS

CHAPTER 11: Fighting Off What's Fighting You: Stress Management

INTRODUCTION

Oh great. One more thing to read in between cramming for that AP test, re-doing the graph for the science lab because my partner forgot to email me the entire data set last night, and typing up the minutes from the last community service club meeting. I have to get all that done before I head off to soccer practice because the play rehearsal is going to be a long one tonight.

Do I really have to read this whole book? Am I going to be tested on it? Isn't there just a summary of the main points somewhere online? Maybe I should just randomly open the book and pick out a deep-sounding quote to throw out to my teacher so it looks like I did the reading. Forget it, I'll just ask my friend tomorrow if there's anything important that I need to know.

Sound familiar?

You learned way back in kindergarten that cheating is wrong, and every year since then, the great teacher vs. student rivalry in the game of

INTRODUCTION

catch-the-cheater has become more and more intense. Students think up sneakier, more creative ways to cheat, and teachers become more advanced cheat-detectors. The penalties are pretty severe, ranging from failing a test all the way to getting a college acceptance withdrawn. With those consequences hanging over your head, why take the risk of cheating? But with all of the pressure on you to ace every single test and participate in a list of activities that is so long, it should have its own study guide, the more obvious question seems to be, why wouldn't you cheat, even given the risks?

You have to make your parents proud, win the approval of your teachers, set yourself up for that perfect future that everyone is always reminding you about, squeeze in some time to see your friends so you don't feel like a total loser, and, oh yeah, try to get more than four hours of sleep per night because lack of sleep and too many energy drink/coffee combos have made your skin look like a pepperoni and sausage pizza. Add in the fact that everywhere you turn, everyone is reminding you how hard it is to get into college these days, and not only do you have to compete with

INTRODUCTION

the other students who can put in an inhuman number of study hours, you also have to deal with the ones who cheat so much they could make a career of it. How are you supposed to impress colleges when you're being compared to all of them? Why shouldn't you cheat just a little bit, too, just to even the playing field?

I could answer that question by telling you the horror stories of students that have failed classes or gotten kicked out of high school or college for cheating. But you know those stories already. Your parents have told you. Your teachers have told you. That annoying kid who always has all the answers in science class has told you. And they don't scare you much, do they? Because for every horror story that you hear, you could probably name ten kids who do cheat and get away with it. Kids who cheated on every test from the twos-times-tables to the AP Chemistry exam and never got caught. Kids who didn't write one original word on one essay throughout high school and got into their first choice college on an English scholarship.

INTRODUCTION

So let's be honest here. Cheating happens. Cheaters often do not get caught. So for just a moment, I'll ignore the issue of getting caught. Switch your brain over from trying to fool your teachers and start thinking about yourself. Cheating does hurt you. It prevents you from ever getting interested in and inspired by what you are supposed to be learning in school because you are more focused on winning the cheating game against the teacher. Cheating also stops you from learning the information and study skills that you are going to need in the future. Eventually, you are going to have to actually know the information without the assistance of a cheat sheet written on the inside of your water bottle label (yeah, teachers are on to that one, too). So many of my freshman college students are shocked by their first test or essay grade of the quarter because they are unprepared for what they have to do in order to succeed in college. Stop (or don't start!) cheating now, and you won't have to worrying about breaking the habit later, when it will be harder. Be kind to your future self. He or she will thank you for it.

INTRODUCTION

But back to reality. We can't ignore the issue of getting caught forever. Many cheaters do get caught. The more often you cheat, the more chances you have of somebody finding out. The consequences are not pleasant. Even if you don't get caught outright at the time, the truth will come out eventually. Think of the athlete who cheats in practice. He might impress the coach momentarily and get to play in the game, but the truth will come out when he can't keep up with the others who spent the time putting in the work at practice.

Instead of the horror stories, I prefer to think of the happy stories. Like the story of one of my clients, a student who had a lot of difficulty with reading and writing, so she was failing English. She had to make up some quizzes on a book that the class was reading, so we spent many hours together reading, analyzing, and making notes on the book. She put in even more time on her own, studying the notes we took. She did so well on the quizzes that the teacher was convinced that she had gotten the questions (and answers) from another student.

INTRODUCTION

The teacher wanted to make an example of her, so he asked her to answer questions about the book in front of the whole class. It is now nearly two years later, and she still loves to relive the story of how she answered every question correctly, even the ones about the most obscure details, how the whole class clapped for her, and how the teacher apologized for doubting her. I don't think she would remember a cheating incident so clearly or so fondly.

I also love the story of one of my college students that failed her first exam of the quarter, and admitted to me that she had cheated on most of her tests throughout high school and her freshman year of college, so she had no clue how to really study for tests that she couldn't cheat on. She spent every week with me during my office hours, working on strategies for really learning the information. She earned A's on the rest of her tests. I even reduced the weight of her first test because I saw the effort that she put in during the rest of the quarter. Plus, I'm a sucker for honesty.

INTRODUCTION

Everyone is always telling you that school is preparing you for the "real world" (whatever that means — as if you're living in a fake world right now). Teachers want you to do everything a certain way because that's what people will expect in college, and then in the workplace. You may not see a connection between a lot of the concepts you have to study in class and what you'll need to know for the rest of your life. Here's a chance to practice real skills in school that will serve you for the rest of your life — both in college and beyond. Skills like standing up for yourself, managing stress, and producing work of which you can be proud.

This book will help you understand yourself by looking at reasons why you might want to cheat. We know there are lots of them! Figuring out why you are tempted to cheat can help you determine the best strategy for avoiding cheating. Don't worry — we'll cover that, too! We'll give you some ideas of what happens to students who are caught cheating, since there may be some horror stories that you haven't heard that might keep you honest. We'll also help you with some of the hardest issues, like dealing with friends who cheat and deciding whether or not to report

cheaters.

Lisa Medoff, Ph.D.

HOW TO USE THIS BOOK

Chill (Relax)

Absorb more information and practical advice.

FOOD FOR THOUGHT

A study conducted by the University of Michigan found that 1/3 of teens feel stressed out on a daily basis. The leading cause? The feeling of not being able to meet high expectations. Prolonged feelings of stress can lead to frustration, illness, aggression, and depression.

Read these inspirational, witty, or tongue-in-cheek observations that you can use to motivate yourself—or just for fun.

Freaking out. Flipping out. Spazzing. Call it what you want, but one thing's for sure: it's not a good thing to do during a test, although it certainly is easy to do!

Maybe you studied more than you've ever studied before and are psyching yourself out that it'll all be for nothing. Maybe you're encountering tougher questions than you expected. Maybe you're wondering if you maybe studied the wrong chapter!

In any case, it won't do you any good to go ballistic. When you're stressing out, you're not thinking clearly and you're more likely to second

A problem is a chance for you to do your best.

—Duke Ellingto

HOW TO USE THIS BOOK

We created the SOS series to help you find answers to questions most pressing on your mind. In developing this series, we brought together both adult and teen experts who shared their successes and struggles. Here's how to best use this book:

...uess your answers and waste more time ...nulling them over than if you're confi- ...ent and calm. So if you find yourself ...weating under the collar, take a second ...o breathe deeply, focus, and chill out. ...'s the best thing you can do for yourself ...uring a test.

F.Y.I.

A few simple ways to manage stress:

1. Positive "Self-Talk" : Try repeating to yourself silently "I can handle this" or "It's going to be O.K." Having a positive attitude can make stress dissapear.

2. See the funny side of life! Look at your situation from a comical perspec- tive and you'll be able to relax, and when you're relaxed you can think more clearly.

DR. LISA SAYS...

When you get the test, take a minute to empty out everything that is cluttering up your brain before you look at any of the questions. Write down all of your mnemonics, formulas, or informa- tion that you're afraid that you'll forget or get confused about. This will not only serve as practical help, but it will also calm you down by focusing you on the information, not on the difficulty of the test. You'll see how much you really do know, and you'll be able to tackle the ques- tions with confidence.

Get expert advice and anecdotes from our series editor, Lisa Medoff, Ph.D.

Absorb more information and practical advice.

HOW TO USE THIS BOOK

Think kids are the only ones who need to learn something? Advice, inside info, and motivation for the know-it-alls in every kid's life.

Look here for basic info and terminology

CHAPTER 12

Fighting Off Wh

What Is It and How Can

PARENT SPEAK

Let's face it, adults know stress. But do you understand how much stress your student is under? A recent poll of high school students revealed that a whopping 70% said that they feel stressed "most of the time." What stress management tools can you share with your kid? Are there experiences you can relate that will help them put things in perspective?

"'m so stressed," is
heard your friend
Recently, you even f
them when they cor
of homework they h
commitments. But w

THE BASICS

stress

n. a specific respon
lus, as fear or pain,
with the normal phy
organism.

physical, mental, or
"Worry over his job
under a great stres

a situation, occurre
"The stress of bein
gave him a poundir

HOW TO USE THIS BOOK

CHAPTER 12

Fighting You: Stress Management

id of It?

u've probably
a daily basis.
iming in with
e mounds
after school
ally??

Stress is the way your body reacts to demands placed on it, whether that's your upcoming advanced Algebra exam or dealing with a difficult friend. When you feel stressed by something, your body releases chemicals into your bloodstream. These chemicals can have both positive and negative effects. Sometimes stress makes you work harder to get something done, but stress can also slow you down, especially if you have no way to deal with the extra energy the chemicals produce in you.

Here, we'll help you understand the causes of stress, signs of stress, how stress affects you, and the best ways to deal with it, because when you've already got so much to do, stress is the last thing you need to worry about.

a stimu-
interferes
rium of an

or tension:
alth put him

sing this:
elevator

FOOD FOR THOUGHT

Many studies suggest that as students get to college, their sleeping schedule suffers greatly. Lack of sleep often results in the inability to concentrate, the need for more naps, and constant fatigue. Try getting a good rest and maybe this will give you more strength to deal with school and other issues.

For fast-acting relief, try slowing down.

——Lily Tomlin

STRESSED OUT
STUDENTS
GUIDE TO
SAYING NO TO
CHEATING

The Heat is On – Why You

> "The pressure is just over-whelming to succeed. It's from my parents, my teachers and, worst of all, myself."

You hear it from the news: There are more and more college applicants every year. You hear it from your parents: You need to get good grades to be competitive when it's time to apply. You hear it from your teachers and school counselors: You need to have a stellar transcript and a laundry list of extracurricular activities if you want to get into the college of your choice.

Sometimes you just want to tell everyone to shut up!

But of course, you don't. You understand that they want you to succeed. What they don't always take into account is how this makes you

THE BASICS

pressure
n. The state of being pressed or compressed. To force (someone) toward a particular end; influence.

Definition from dictionary.com

Might Want to Cheat

feel when you're trying your hardest and still falling behind.

You get scared.

You start to get desperate.

You start to consider cheating.

Whoa, there! Not so fast. Where desperation threatens to set in, logic must prevail. Let's dig right into the issue of cheating, and where the pressure to do it comes from.

I think some of the pressure comes from the expectations of other people. Like if your father played baseball, they expect you to be the big lifesaver or something when you play a sport.

—Barry Bonds

FOOD FOR THOUGHT

From homework, to sports and extra-curricular activities, there's not enough time in the day to do it all—and what about your friends? Try to get organized, either on your computer or paper. It's easier to fit things in if you can find a space here or there.

The Man (Pressure From Your School)

Technically, the school's goal is to discourage you from cheating. When you're studying so much that you're not sure you'll ever see the light of day, however, you start to consider your options for shortcuts.

Unfortunately for you, blaming the system isn't going to fly with the principal of the school as an excuse for why the answers to a test were taped on a piece of paper to the underside of your baseball cap brim.

FOOD FOR THOUGHT

A Rutgers University professor reported in 2008 that a study revealed 95% of high school students admit to have cheated during the course of their education.

PARENT SPEAK

Unfortunately, the pressure to excel at school often outweighs common sense or ethics. Everyone wants to succeed and no one wants to be left behind. How can you help your child do well and maintain their integrity?

Maybe you know plenty of your peers who have already bowed to the pressure they faced at school, and are cheating regularly. Maybe you've had one or two opportunities to join them. Have you resisted? Or do you now need to return from the Dark Side?

If you've cheated, ask yourself how it makes you feel? Is the pressure so great that you just want to get through the class, or are you disappointed that you didn't struggle to make it on your own?

> If you're not at the top of the class, there's a feeling that you just shouldn't be there. The teachers don't say it, but you can feel it.

DR. LISA SAYS...

Colleges know that you cannot possibly have participated in 10 clubs, 5 sports, and 500 hours of community service while taking every AP course the school has to offer. They are looking for someone who is passionate about and committed to one or two activities, not someone who showed up to one meeting to get her name on the sign-in sheet. Instead of trying to get on the roster of every club in school, immerse yourself in the activities that are the most rewarding to you. You might actually enjoy your life and look good to colleges at the same time.

(Pressure From Colleges)

Your school's intention is not to give you so much work that you resort to cheating. That said, their curriculum is designed to be challenging enough so that the stars among you will shine. Why? Because colleges have a decision to make, and they'll be looking for the students that separate themselves from the pack. But of course, you already know this.

You're probably sick of hearing about college. Your parents are on your case about it, your

FOOD FOR THOUGHT

Cheating isn't always motivated by lack of morals. Other reasons teens cheat are insecurity, a quest for perfection, laziness, and a desire to please their parents, all of which override their better judgment.

Yes, I cheat. Everyone cheats at my school and the teachers have to know about it. I mean, really, how many A's can a teacher give out before he gets suspicious.

school counselors and teachers always insist on reminding you, and as application time rolls around, the colleges and universities themselves are also going to be filling your mailbox with brochures.

Sometimes it may seem like you're being pitted against your classmates in a giant rat race, trying to get that big, stinky cheese that is the college acceptance letter. But even in a rat race, you have to run the maze to deserve your prize. You get no points for hopping the walls.

> " If you don't quit, and don't cheat, and don't run home when trouble arrives, you can only win. "
>
> ——Shelley Long

DR. LISA SAYS...

People can become obsessed with getting into the highest-ranked, most prestigious college. I always tell students that it is more important to find a place where you fit in and where you will be happy for four years of your life. Why scam your way into a school where you'll just feel like you have to keep cheating in order to survive? You'll be signing up for another four years of guaranteed frustration and misery. Why not find a school that suits your own academic style and talents?

(Pressure From Friends and Classmates)

They may be your friends, you may like them a whole lot, but they are also your competition... as the school won't let you forget.

We all know about the bell curve; typically (and theoretically) only a small fraction of students can get an A in a class, a larger proportion will get Bs and Cs, and there will be a number of students who do worse than that, close or equal to the number of A-getters.

The ugly reality is that peer pressure reaches its greatest intensity at just the age when kids tend to be most insensitive and cruel.

—Walt Mueller,
Understanding Today's Youth Culture

In this climate, you may feel like you have to claw your way and step on some heads to get to the top. Up against so many of your peers for the same prizes, you may do drastic things to make sure you get ahead.

On the flip side of things, you may be less of a fighter and more of a giver. Surely, some of your friends have asked you for "help" on homework assignments they didn't do, or tests they didn't study for. Maybe this has been you, on especially desperate or lazy days.

Either way, your friends and classmates provide plenty of pressure to cheat, and plenty of opportunities too.

DR. LISA SAYS...

When it comes to fudging information on your college applications, always assume the worst. Sure, it's likely that the college won't find out if you exaggerated the number of community service hours that you did or if you were really vice-president of the chess club. However, admissions officers are quite aware of all of the tricks that students use to try to get into their schools, and they may very well be spot-checking claims. Don't risk it! Besides, schools take a lot of things into consideration when looking at your application, and there is a miniscule chance that your acceptance will hinge on your number of community service hours alone.

(Pressure From Parents)

DR. LISA SAYS...

From your parents' point of view:

Your parents may never admit it, but all parents make mistakes when it comes to raising children. However, you should understand that almost every mistake really comes from a place of good intentions. Parents want the best for their children, and sometimes they can be so blinded by this desire that they don't see how the pressure that they are putting on you is hurting you. If they are pushing you to succeed, it is because they think that getting good grades and going to a great college will make you happy and secure for the rest of your life.

Most of our parents would never want or ask us to cheat. But sometimes, when they push us to do whatever it takes to be successful, we can tend to get mixed messages. Chances are, you've never sat your mom and dad down and asked the question:

"Which is more important to you? That I try my best and fail? Or that I find some way to succeed at any cost?"

You don't want to disappoint your parents; that's a given. And let's face it: sometimes making them proud yields some pretty sweet rewards.

So do your parents give you pressure to cheat? Most definitely they do, even if it's inadvertentl. And if your parents are telling you to cheat straight up, it sounds like your parents, though they mean well, have lost sight of their priorities for your education.

But most parents really do have your best interest at heart—they just want you to succeed in this increasingly competitive world. As silly as it sounds, the best way to combat this pressure is to talk to them...all the time. If they don't hear you the first time, keep saying it. One day it'll get through, loud and clear.

> If my Mom would just back off a little bit, then maybe I could actually get something from this (class). But I get so many questions about my grades, and studying, that I feel like that's all she cares about.

DR. LISA SAYS...

If your parents' expectations for you are stressing you out, talk to them. Start out by telling them specifically how you are feeling. Stay calm and don't accuse them of anything – just keep it about you. Take some time before you talk to them to think about how you will explain to them what you are feeling, exactly what in your life is stressing you out, and the things that you need them to do in order to help you. They may not agree to everything, but they will hear you. If you don't feel that you can remain calm in a discussion, write them a note or an email.

(Pressure From Yourself)

The greatest pressure to cheat sometimes comes from yourself. You take all the pressure in from the various outside sources and decide whether you want to do things honorably, or find a shortcut that is... less honest.

The key to not cheating is knowing that you have the strength to handle the pressure. You don't have to give yourself over to something you know is wrong and potentially very damaging. If you need help or convincing, we've got you covered here. Read on.

FOOD FOR THOUGHT

What are the biggest causes of pressure for students?

1. School

2. Peer Relationships

3. Family

4. Fear of Failure

"All good is hard. All evil is easy. Dying, losing, cheating, and mediocrity is easy. Stay away from easy."

—Scott Alexander

It may start off very innocently. You've got a couple of tests or papers due back to back. You're feeling overwhelmed and so is everyone around you. A classmate suggests an easy "solution". It doesn't feel right, but it'll dig you out of this hole. But then there's another situation. Before you know it, you're caught in a dangerous game.

DR. LISA SAYS...

Sometimes the worst pressure can come from inside of you. You've taken all of the expectations that everyone has had of you over the years, and bottled it up inside you. It's really hard to let that go! I can't tell you to go easy on yourself – that just won't happen, will it? But I can tell you to try to stop setting yourself up with all-or-nothing thinking. That means that you need to stop telling yourself that anything other than an A+ (no matter how it is achieved) is failure.

> "My dad, who owns his own company, always says he's his own worst boss. Now I'm starting to understand what that means—no one is harder on me than me."

"Everybody's Doing It" – Why Y

> I didn't think there was anything wrong with it. We were all sharing answers and it seemed like the only way to get all our projects done.

Classes and grades aside, the life of a teenager is just packed with things to worry about, you know? Of course you know.

You're still learning about who you are and what you're capable of. You're handling social pressures – girlfriends, boyfriends, backstabbing, friendships, etc. Plus, you've got all the

DR. LISA SAYS...

Talk with your teachers at the first sign of trouble. Don't let things pile up until you get so far behind that you can't possibly catch up without cheating. If you're having trouble getting started on an essay, meet with your teacher to brainstorm possible ideas a week ahead of time, rather than waiting until the last minute when you're so frustrated that you turn to plagiarism. Don't understand the math? Ask your teacher for daily homework help, rather than trying to cram the night before the test, and then turning to cheating when cramming doesn't work.

r Friends Might Want to Cheat

things you care about—sports, clubs, hobbies, dances, and parties—to take your mind off of school, grades, and tests.

Sometimes it may feel like with everything you've got going on, there's just no time for all the things your school wants you to focus on. Or maybe you actually have been putting in all the time, and you still aren't performing in your classes as well as you'd like.

Then, along come opportunities to cheat in order to get ahead, or simply to leave you time to do whatever you find more interesting than homework (let's face it; that's probably most things).

Many people take the bait. It can get to the point where you think, "what's the big deal? Why not? Everybody's doing it!"

But DON'T!

Let's look at the reasons people cheat, and figure out how you can sidestep or rise above them.

FOOD FOR THOUGHT

The results of a survey reported by CNN revealed that 50% of 4,500 students polled didn't think that copying questions and answers from a test is actually cheating.

Caving In (Because the Pressure Has Gotte

PARENT SPEAK

When your kid seems panicked about a test or assignment, don't tell yourself that it's a passing thing. Find out the "what" and "why" of the problem and see if you can draw on your experiences to give some sage advice—or at least an ear to listen.

F or most people, the decision to cheat is not one that's taken lightly... at least not the first time.

It could be a homework assignment that has been kicking your butt up and down the block, or a difficult chapter in a textbook that you've read over and over and still can't understand. It could be a long period of personal troubles, or an activity that has been taking up all your time. In any case, when the C's and D's start stacking up, you start to feel the pressure.

The class was pretty treacherous—I probably could have conquered it if I didn't already have a full schedule. Cheating was my only option.

o Them)

The threat of failure in a class is reason enough for teens who look forward to a bright future to panic. Ultimately, panic brings moments of weakness, and it is in these moment that you do things that you know are wrong.

...and then I did it again. And again.

DR. LISA SAYS...

Honesty goes a long way with many teachers. One student that I work with was having trouble finishing a huge, multi-part assignment by the due date. She initially wanted to stay home from school or give the teacher an excuse, but we decided that she had to turn in the parts that were finished, tell the truth, and accept the consequences. The teacher was incredibly frustrated with the many other students who gave excuses about why their projects were not done, and she was so impressed by the student's honesty that she granted her the only extension in the class.

Acting Out (Because They're Angry at the

FOOD FOR THOUGHT

60.8% of college students surveyed have cheated. Of students who cheat, only 16.5% feel bad about it.

Will Smith said it back in his "Fresh Prince" days, and you probably agree: "Parents just don't understand." In fact you'd probably like to add some more adults to that list. Teachers just don't understand. School administrators just don't understand.

It can be hard to be a teen, and when you're dealing with your own issues and the issues of your friends, sometimes the sheer volume of homework or the glut of tests you have to take seem unnecessary. Why does everything have to be so hard when you're already facing so much?

We didn't mean to steal a copy of the test, but we saw it sticking out under some papers on our teacher's desk. He left his office, I stuffed it under my shirt, and voila! The easiest A I ever got.

chool and Their Teachers)

Teens who are going through especially hard times might take a little joy or pride in cheating because they feel like they are beating a system that seems "unfair" or "harsh". Their acts of rebellion however, can easily come back to bite them.

WHAT DO YOU DO?

Your math teacher's tests are unfair and everyone knows it. They are unnecessarily hard, they feature questions that weren't even covered in class OR in the textbook… how the heck is anyone supposed to get an A?

Your friend has a way. After school he snuck into the classroom and copied the answers to the next test, right out of a copy that was in the teacher's desk. He's offering to share.

DR. LISA SAYS…

It is unavoidable. You will have teachers that are bad, mean, unfair, or just don't like you for some strange reason. So it is understandable that you will be angry with them. You may even want to cheat just to get back at them. But don't risk it. Think about how those unfair teachers may give really extreme punishments if they catch you cheating. Instead, deal with the problem. Talk with the teacher first to see if there is anything you can do differently in order to succeed in his or her class. If that doesn't work, and you really feel that you are being mistreated, make an appointment to speak with the administration.

The Bait (Because They Had an "Opportunity")

It's twenty minutes until the start of third period and you haven't done your homework. Why? Something stupid, like a Twilight Zone marathon on TV, or just plain forgetfulness. But you're already floundering in the class, and a missed homework assignment might just tip you over into the red zone.

"Hey," says your friend, "Chill. Just copy mine."

When the stakes are high and the chances of getting caught are low, a lot of teens will succumb to temptation. The problem is, once you do it once, it gets easier every time thereafter. Before

FOOD FOR THOUGHT

A poll conducted by Junior Achievement found that 38% of teens believe it is sometimes "necessary" to cheat, plagiarize, lie, or use violence to succeed.

Look at the other things grouped in with "to cheat" and decide for yourself if it's a good thing.

> It is impossible for a man to be cheated by anyone but himself.
>
> ——Ralph Waldo Emerson

you know it, you're rarely ever doing your own work, and that's a dangerous way to be.

As frustrating as school can be, the goal is to learn how to learn. If you're just learning how to cheat, you're selling yourself short. You already know that you should have spent that time doing your homework instead of watching TV, or that you should be keeping track of your assignments in a daily planner, so let this time be a lesson to you and get it done next time!

F.Y.I.

Students who cheat their way through high school and even college often do not stop cheating even after they graduate. In fact, according to the Educational Testing Service organization, résumé fraud is a major concern of many employers looking to hire students straight from college.

Yeah, I don't really buy into that 'everyone else is doing it' thing. BUT, when everyone else is cheating, it's the only way to stay competitive. And competition is what it's all about.

The Switch (Because They Wanted to Fit

PARENT SPEAK

When peer pressure hits the boiling (or cheating) point, don't get angry and/or point fingers at your students' friends when you should be challenging your own child. It's often easier to scapegoat a seemingly bad or misguided kid than address the issues that are challenging your own.

Y our friends are important to you, and they should be. They've got your back when things get hot, and you can always lean on them when things aren't going so well for you. You know you'd do the same for them; if they need your help, you're there in a heartbeat. You stick together.

So what happens when someone in your group of friends gets their hands on the answers to a test and decides that they'll do a public service by sharing?

Don't think you're on the right road just because it's a well-beaten path.

—Unknown

th Others)

While everyone enthusiastically gathers around, you have to wonder... how many of them would have resisted the urge to look if the "opportunity" hadn't been presented as a "group activity?"

HALL OF SHAME

Milli Vanilli was a pop and dance group featuring Fab Morvan and Rob Pilatus. Their debut album won a Grammy Award in 1990, and with over 30 million singles and 14 million albums sold, the group's frontmen were on top of the world.

Then it was discovered that they not only had lip-synced all their performances, but that the vocals on their album had been recorded by someone else. The media backlash was fierce. The Grammy was taken from them and their careers were ruined. Rob later suffered major depression and took his own life in 1998 with a drug overdose.

"It was my friend's idea, but it wouldn't work unless we all did it together. So we did. And we all got caught. Together."

Dumb (Because They Feel "Stupid")

FOOD FOR THOUGHT

Junior Achievement Worldwide discovered in a poll that 44% of teens say they feel either a lot or overwhelming pressure to succeed.

Have you ever seen one of those pictures that looks like abstract impressionist art—only when you hold it up to your nose and then take it slowly away, then try to unfocus and look into the distance... you should be seeing a floating 3D image?

Have you ever not been able to see the 3D bunny or mug of coffee or genie's lamp or whatever?

That's pretty much what it feels like when you study and study or work and work and still just

"Two things are infinite: the universe and human stupidity; and I'm not sure about the universe."

—Albert Einste

can't understand a subject or assignment. You may have access to the answer and think, "Why not? It's not like I didn't try or put the work in! Shouldn't I get an A for effort?"

Sometimes doing things the conventional way just doesn't work. Everyone learns and studies differently and just because you try very hard to study one way doesn't guarantee results. Sometimes you have to try different ways to find what works best for you. Then the time you spend will really be valuable and your effort will be rewarded, hopefully with an A!

F.Y.I.

According to the Gallup Organization (October 6-9, 2000), the top two problems facing the country today are: 1) Education and 2) Decline in Ethics (both were ranked over crime, poverty, drugs, taxes, guns, environment, and racism, to name a few).

> " Yeah, it seemed like a good idea at the time. No matter how much I studied, I couldn't understand the concept. Cheating seemed like my only choice. "

Dumber (Because They Wanted to Avoid †

FOOD FOR THOUGHT

Recent studies have shown that not only does technology make cheating easier, it also blurs the lines between "research" and "cheating." Once the lines are blurred, it makes it much quicker for bad habits to take root and erode good study habits.

You know the kind of person who never does his or her own work? Who's made it a morning ritual to find someone to bum some homework answers off of in the morning before class? Who's always asking classmates for permission to copy off of their tests because he/she "forgot" to study the night before?

We hope you're not one of them!

Some people have gotten into the habit of being lazy, and this is the worst, most idiotic, and most

"Laziness may appear attractive, but work gives satisfaction."

—Anne Frank

Work)

self-destructive reason to cheat of all the ones you can think of. People who have fallen into this pattern have hard lives ahead of them, unless they can snap out of it now and pick up some work ethic.

You might laugh now, but cheating does catch up with you—even if you never get caught. At some point, you'll be expected to put your hard studying to work and, well, what do you think happens then?

> I just didn't want to do the work. Period. Nothing more to it.

DR. LISA SAYS...

Being lazy will hurt you eventually, and the earlier you try to stop the pattern of getting out of work, the easier it will be to acquire good study habits. Set easy goals, like getting just your math homework done before settling in on the couch for the afternoon. Take small steps, like telling yourself that you are just going to work really hard on your own for this one project or exam — no cheating. Get a taste of what it feels like to work for something and feel the pride of your effort paying off.

Burn! – What Happen

> I never even thought I could get caught. I thought it was the worst-kept secret on campus.

As you can see, there's an entire world of reasons teens are pressured or lured into cheating for the first time, and to continue cheating after that. Though there are moral and philosophical arguments against cheating, let's just say it out loud: the most convincing deterrent to cheating is knowledge of what the immediate consequences will be. And though they're not the most fun things to discuss, knowing about them is important if you want to effectively talk yourself out of getting involved in a bad situation

F.Y.I.

Common punishments for cheating at school:

✓ A failing grade
✓ Detention
✓ Suspension
✓ Phone call to parents
✓ Mark on your permanent record

When You Get Caught

Sometimes the consequences aren't immediate, which makes cheating seem harmless and freeing from all the pressures of studying and working hard. But it does, and will, catch up with you. And when it does, the results are painful.

The consequences of cheating clearly outweigh any benefit you thought you were getting, as you will see in plentiful example here. Read on!

> Do they think we're stupid or something?
>
> ——Mr. Elser, 6th grade math teacher

DR. LISA SAYS...

Teachers may seem oblivious sometimes, but they're not stupid. They were students at one point, too, and they may have even cheated a few times themselves. They have also dealt with hundreds of students a day for many years, so they know what to look out for. They get suspicious when you do things like hand in homework that is always correct and then totally bomb the test. And one more piece of insider information: Even if they don't call you on it this time, it doesn't mean they haven't noticed. Sometimes teachers will wait for more concrete evidence, or an opportunity to catch you in a more serious incident.

Red-Handed (Academic Consequences)

HALL OF SHAME

In 2008, six sophomores at Harvard-Westlake—a prestigious, top-performing Los Angeles private school—were expelled and more than a dozen other students faced suspensions when it was discovered they conspired and stole Spanish and history midterm tests and passed them around.

Let's cut to the chase.

Your junior high or high school likely has some pretty harsh punishments for cheating. You could be facing hours of detention when you have much better things to do with your time. That disciplinary action for cheating on your academic record won't make things easy for you for a good long while, as we'll discuss here soon enough.

"I generally assume that someone in my class is cheating...even when there's no grade involved. I think it's become a habit."

—Dr. Glaser, 11th grade AP Chemistry

Taking a longer view however, cheating liter-
ally cheats you out of the knowledge that
should be rightfully yours. While others are
learning and retaining information in a way
that will allow them to use it to score better
on standardized tests and be more effective
and intelligent communicators, you'll have
deprived yourself of the learning process, and
for something as insignificant in the long run
as a better score or letter grade.

F.Y.I.

**Consequences for cheating
can include:**

✓ F grade for project/test
✓ F grade for class
✓ Incomplete, must repeat class
✓ Ineligibility to play sports/extracurricular
  activities
✓ Suspension
✓ Expulsion

"I can't believe I have to repeat the class. And, I can't go to prom. I didn't think it was a big deal."

They're Onto You (Ramifications for Colleg

HALL OF SHAME

In 2007, thirty-four students at the prestigious Duke University business administration school were found guilty of cheating on a take-home test. 9 were expelled, 15 were suspended for a whole year, and 9 were failed from the course. Only 4 were cleared of the charges altogether.

If it's still not clear why getting caught cheating can really mess you up, get ready. Here comes the doozy.

One of the biggest, if not the biggest red flags on a student record that prompts colleges to bypass an applicant is a history of cheating. The reason for this is that a great concern of colleges is turning out students who are prepared to do their own scholarship and contribute original ideas to the field. Plagiarism is the ultimate no-no in every college class, and the most obvious predictor

"The first and worst of all frauds is to cheat one's self."

—Pearl Baile

of a college plagiarist is a high school cheater.

So if you still think that cheating is no big deal, consider for a moment that to colleges, it is a very big deal, and then decide whose opinion might mean a little bit more when it comes to your future.

F.Y.I.

It's often said that cheaters never prosper, but is that really true?

In an exclusive ABCNEWS Primetime poll of 12- to 17-year-olds, seven in 10 say at least some kids in their school cheat on tests. Six in 10 have friends who've cheated. About one in three say they themselves have cheated, rising to 43 percent of older teens. And most say cheaters don't get caught.

> I was admitted to 6 of the 11 universities I applied to during early admission. After my final transcripts were sent that showed I had cheated, I was lucky to convince 1 school to take me—and I was on immediate academic probation, which sucks for a freshman.

Can't Shake It (Social Consequences)

Getting caught cheating sucks for many reasons, and on top of all of those, there are the social consequences. When you're worried about getting that good grade at all costs, what your friends will think of you may be the last thing on your mind. How would you feel, however, if you knew that one of your classmates got a better grade on an assignment than you did after cheating? Angry right? Now imagine the cheater is you.

FOOD FOR THOUGHT

Why do so many teens think that cheating is no big deal? In 200, the Josephson's Institute of Ethics found that 34% of teens said their parents never talked to them about cheating.

"There may not be a permanent record, but there's definitely an ongoing record. We keep track of who the cheaters are and how they're doing in classes."

— Ms. Taub, 9th grade English

Cheating can cost you friendships—both the ones you have and the ones you would have made if you didn't have a reputation as a cheater. Few people want to risk their own credibility by being associated with a known cheater (would they be implicated as an accomplice if you were caught in a cheating scheme, they might wonder), and no one wants to run the risk of being pressured to give up hard-earned notes or answers.

And if you think your teachers are above gossip, think again. Just as most people would, they warn each other about cheaters they've caught and they brag about catching them. If you think your classes are hard now, think of how hard they'll be when the teacher already has a bad impression of you and your work from the very beginning.

You've heard that people's reputations precede them. When you're a cheater, this truism spells major, major disaster.

> "I was caught cheating off a friend's paper last year. Now all the teachers think I'm cheating all the time."

Hero For a Day – Talkin

> " I got caught cheating last year, only I wasn't cheating. It took some help from my counselor and my dad, but I was able to defend myself. After that, I'm done with (not) cheating. "

You like your friends because you know in your heart that they're good people. You wouldn't (or shouldn't) like them otherwise. And contrary to what you might think at first, cheaters aren't always bad people: they are experiencing a moment of weakness or several moments of bad judgment.

When these people who you know are good are about to make bad decisions, you are the most help when you can talk them out of it. Keeping them from becoming down and out is even better than being there for them when they're hitting bottom.

F.Y.I.

A professor at Arizona State University found that "74 percent of employees say they've seen someone at work do something unethical or illegal—but most say they would never report such acts to supervisors."

People Out of Cheating

When you know about some cheating that's about to go down, your instinct should be to do what you can to talk your friend or classmate *out of it.*

While it might be difficult to approach your friend and tell them that you think they're doing something wrong, remind yourself, and them, that you're doing it because you care about them and you don't want them to do something they will regret later.

> Fool me once, shame on you. Fool me twice, shame on me.
>
> —Unknown.

DR. LISA SAYS...

Why would you want to talk someone out of cheating? You can think about it from a selfish point of view. If someone else is cheating, it might blow the curve for you, and you'll end up with a lower grade. The teacher might catch your friend, and assume that you are a cheater, as well, since you two hang out together. You can even just look at it as a chance to practice your skills of persuasion – challenge yourself to be able to talk your friend out of cheating. You can also take a more generous viewpoint – you might be saving your friend from some very bad consequences.

Great Power (Arguments You Can Use)

FOOD FOR THOUGHT

Nearly all teens in a national, random-sample survey said cheating's wrong. Most who admitted to cheating say it was a rare thing. And fewer than three in 10 said "most" or "a lot" of kids in their school cheat; 44 percent said it's just "some."

Someone admits to you that he or she is going to employ some questionable methods to score well on homework or on a test. The very fact that that person has told you means that you're a trusted confidant, and your opinion matters to that person. The best thing you can do for this person is to talk him or her out of what can end up being a big mistake. Here are some effective arguments to pull out of your utility belt.

"Are you sure you won't get caught? Are you sure sure? If you're not, you better not risk it."

"Hey, I studied/worked for hours on that and sorry, but it just isn't fair to me if you cheat."

Sometimes we cheat on a test when the score doesn't even affect our grade. We just do it because that's what we do.

"I heard cheating ruins your chances of getting into college. Seriously."

"Well, what's the worst thing that can happen if you don't do it? So you get a bad grade... big whoop."

...there are a million other arguments you can surely come up with on your own!

HALL OF SHAME

12-year-old Danny Almonte was Little League sensation. In the summer of 2001, he pitched a perfect game for the Baby Bronx Bombers and garnered significant media attention.

It was soon discovered however, that he was, in fact, 14 years old and had lied to officials. Though he could really pitch a 70 mph fastball, none of that mattered to anyone anymore. His father, who had forged his registration form, was banned from the Little League for life.

> "Do the right thing. It will gratify some people and astonish the rest."
>
> —Mark Twain

Great Responsibility (Leveraging Yo

FOOD FOR THOUGHT

Cheating is universally appalling, and has been for all of history. There's a very old saying that goes: "Cheaters never win, and winners never cheat."

W hen you think of all the things you can be saving a would-be cheater from by talking him or her out of it, you'll realize you can be a hero, and your friendship is your greatest weapon.

You can spare your friend the agony of being caught and reprimanded for cheating. Even if he or she gets away with it the first time, it's a slippery slope and cheating once can easily lead to repeat performances (where the risk of being caught is there every time). Being branded a

"I couldn't tell, because she was my friend. But there were others in class that had no problem telling."

riendship)

cheater in any official or unofficial way leads to trouble aplenty. You may feel as if you have to leverage your friendship to snap him or her out of it:

"I didn't know you could be so dishonest. This would definitely change the way I see you, and that sucks."

"I don't think we should be hanging out as much, since teachers are going to see you as a cheater and lump me in with you."

"Why didn't you just ask me to help you study (or explain those questions)? You know I would have. Just take your hits this time on this test/assignment, and I'll help you get your grade back up with a study session for the next test, alright?"

"Missing some questions on this test isn't the end of the world, but cheating could be. It's just not worth it."

"Important principles may and must be inflexible."

—Abraham Lincoln

Great Reward (What's in It For You)

WHAT TO DO?

You discover that a friend of yours is planning to cheat on a test, and try as you might, you can't talk her out of it.

Later on in the day, you get a call to the principal's office. Your friend has been caught, and she's pointed the finger at you as being the one who gave her the answers to the test.

It's a pretty good feeling, at the end of the day or the end of your high school years, to know that everything you got, you got honestly. It's an even better feeling to know that along the way, you were able to help your friends stay on track as well.

Respect is often not something you start out with. In school, at home, and in your future workplace, it's something you earn from your peers. After you've talked your friends out of cheating during a moment of weakness, you can

" When you are content to be simply yourself and don't compare or compete, everybody will respect you. "

—Lao Tzu

be sure they'll look back on the incident when they're more clear-headed and think the world of you . And if not, it's their loss, not yours.

Friends that stick by you and try to help you make the right decisions even when things get hard are the ones you want to hang on to. It's the kind of friend you'd want, and the kind of friend you want to be.

PARENT SPEAK

How do you advise your child to stand up for him or herself when there's cheating going on? You've learned that someone always gets hurt, but your student may see cheating as a victimless crime. Find a way to acknowledge and validate your child's concerns about his or her relationships with friends and peers, and try to remember how important your friendships were at that point in your life.

> " I don't care what the other kids say or do. I'm going to do what's right for me and my future—well, maybe I care a little. "

On the Case – Reporting

"Some-times kids tell on the cheat-ers even though they cheat them-selves. That's not so good."

When you find out that a classmate of yours is planning to cheat on an assignment or test, it's so easy to just dismiss it. After all, it's their problem if they can't do things honestly like everyone else, right?

But that's wrong. So wrong. Cheaters artificially inflate grades in classes and in schools, and they screw up the "curve." Cheaters aren't just cheating the teachers or the school system. They are

F.Y.I.

Saving a Would-Be Cheater, Tip #1

If your friend goes through a period of being very stressed out over tests, and then becomes noticeably less concerned about studying, it's time to be upfront and have a talk with him/her. They might have started relying on a cheating method, and the longer they do it, the more of a habit it becomes.

Cheaters

cheating you, your friends, and any of your other classmates who do things legitimately.

When you know that a cheater has done better than you on a test, it's little consolation sometimes to be able to say "It's okay, I still have my principles" if your good principles aren't helping you and others like you get ahead of people who have no principles in this respect.

We know you've been taught since grade school that "tattling" is a bad thing, but you're not in grade school anymore. As a teen, your judgment is good enough to tell you when you're "telling on" someone just to be self-righteous, and when you're reporting something that you know is wrong. In the big picture, you're doing a public service.

FOOD FOR THOUGHT

According to the Educational Testing Service, high school students are less likely to report a cheating friend than younger students due to the fright of being called unpopular or a "tattle-tale."

Have the courage to say no. Have the courage to face the truth. Do the right thing because it is right. These are the magic keys to living your life with integrity.

——W. Clement Stone

Eye Witness (When You See It Happening

DR. LISA SAYS...

You don't have to call out the cheater right in the middle of the test. You can always talk to the teacher in private or write a note on your test about what you saw. You can even put an anonymous note in her box in the office or slip the note into the pile of tests being turned in. You don't even have to accuse anyone specifically – you can just warn the teacher that you suspect cheating was taking place, and tell her to be extremely careful in grading the tests.

An accusation can be an ugly thing, but when you catch someone who's undeniably engaged in the act of cheating, a well-placed look of disapproval can stop the cheater right in his or her tracks without a single word. What better deterrent for someone who's trying not to get caught than a clear indication that they've been caught?

If you see it happening but have no way of gracefully stopping it as it is, your next move is a delicate one. We've established that there's a difference between tattling and reporting a crime. However, some of your classmates (especially ones with guilty consciences) may subscribe to a prison-based mentality when it comes to your reporting.

" Betrayal is the only truth that sticks. "

—Arthur Miller

"Nobody likes a rat."

But you are not a rat. If anything, you're a witness. To borrow from the movie "Mean Girls", "There are two kinds of evil people: people who do evil stuff, and people who see evil stuff being done and don't try to stop it." Talk to a teacher afterwards and in private if you have to in order to prevent "evil stuff being done."

DR. LISA SAYS...

 Be very thoughtful before making any type of accusation. Consider all of the possible consequences, both for the alleged cheater and for yourself. If you suspect cheating, but don't have proof, you may just have to let it go this time and be on the lookout next time. Remember, it is ultimately the teacher's job to worry about cheaters. If you are concerned, you may just want to approach the teacher about altering testing situations or about being more alert regarding specific types of cheating.

> I hate being stuck in the middle. Cheaters ruin the curve for everyone, but I don't want to be the one to turn them in.

A Sneaking Suspicion (If You Suspect It)

As we've said, an accusation is never pretty, but that's especially true if it's a false one. It's easy to be zealous about identifying and reporting cheaters, especially if your own grade or score on the assignment/test in question was disappointing, and you feel the injustice of the whole situation.

Catching and reporting a cheater can take on the life of a witch-hunt in a way, because everyone

FOOD FOR THOUGHT

A recent study of several hundred high school students revealed that many students began cheating because they thought their friends did it, or other students bragged about it.

Kids talk. And they believe each others' stories. Sometimes it's true, sometimes it's not. I try to look at every student individually.

—Mr. Peters, middle school vice principal

who didn't cheat will feel directly wronged by the person who cheated. That's why it's important, if you have a sneaking suspicion, to talk to the person directly before spreading the rumor and letting a mob of classmates decide the person's guilt based on a scrap of information. Given how damaging claims of cheating can be, situations like this must be handled with finesse.

F.Y.I.

Saving a Would-Be Cheater, Tip #2

If your grade isn't in danger but some of your friends' are, you might get left out of cheating schemes by your friends. Don't be hurt if it looks like you're being left out of it, but don't let them get away with it without letting them know that you don't approve, and you'd prefer it if they would just let you help them study.

"Everyone was talking about how my friend was copying the answers for our English exam. When I asked her, it turned out the teacher had given her a separate test for make up. She wasn't cheating at all."

Insider Info (If You Hear About It)

PARENT SPEAK

If your student tells you about a classmate that may be cheating, try not to jump to any conclusions or pass any value judgments. Encourage your kid to speak with their friend and use this opportunity to reinforce the positive behaviors you expect.

Similarly, it's probably not the best choice to immediately go blabbing it to your class-mates or to a school administrator without actual evidence when you get a "tip" that someone cheated. Even in a real U.S. court of law, "hear-say" doesn't hold up as reason to find someone guilty of a crime, no matter how credible the source.

Again, confront the person directly and candidly

When I hear about what other kids are doing, I don't know whether I feel left out or am glad that I'm not caught up in it.

first so he or she can do damage control if it's an unfounded rumor. And if that person has actually cheated, he or she will know that it's hard to completely escape notice. They'll think twice before doing it again next time.

If that person is a friend, you can ask him or her directly. Try to listen and not place blame. There may be a reason for their behavior, or some way you can help. Try to make it about their story, not your agenda.

Sometimes, there has been a misunderstanding or a mis-read of the situation. Other times, the rumors may be dead-on, but there's an opportunity to turn a negative situation into a positive.

F.Y.I.

Saving a Would-Be Cheater, Tip #3

If you know your friend is cheating regularly, try everything you can to help them break the habit before you resort to threatening to alert the school. You have more power to influence him/her in the right ways over time if you do what you can to preserve your friendship.

Oh No! – Drawbacks of

> "Everyone talks about your 'permanent record' but there's really no such thing."

You know it's wrong. You know why people do it, even though it's wrong. You know what the immediate academic consequences are if you get caught.

But do you know how cheating can affect you in the long run?

HALL OF SHAME

The East German Olympic team were the darlings of world athletics in the 1970s through the 80s. Though the country had fewer than 17 million people, it seemed to be turning out athletes that could really give the US and Soviet Union teams a run for their money.

It later came to light that trainers and coaches had doped their athletes with banned steroids, telling them that they were vitamins. Many of these athletes, unfortunately, suffered from health problems like organ damage or hormonal changes.

Cheating

Our society takes cheating very seriously. Laws are built around preventing or discouraging the actions of cheaters... people who cheat other people out of their money, people who cheat other people out of happiness or life. Not to be dramatic or anything, but criminals are just advanced cheaters, if you really think about it!

Here are just a few more things to think about, so you can look at cheating in the right context—the context that matters the most to you:

Your life.

Cheating is the one thing that follows you throughout your entire academic career. No matter what anyone says, it's a career killer.

—Joe, college admissions counselor

FOOD FOR THOUGHT

3 Reasons Not to Cheat

1. It's wrong.

2. It's stupid.

3. You're better than that.

Not Good (You Hurt Yourself)

DR. LISA SAYS...

One major way that you hurt yourself is through the anxiety that often comes with cheating. You will probably feel worried about getting caught, which can disrupt your sleep the night before the test, and then distract you throughout the day. You might even keep worrying for weeks afterward about whether the teacher will suddenly find out or if a classmate will tell on you. On the other hand, if you cheat enough and get away with it, you might stop worrying, which is exactly when you will get cocky about it and get caught!

If you've ever had to read Les Miserables, you know that the title character, Jean Valjean, works for years and years to get his life back on track after he's derailed it by being a thief. Now, our pal Jean had a very good reason for thieving in the first place (dude was hungry), but it didn't change the fact that when he was freed from jail, he had a host of nasty habits he had to break, and a lot of people in his life who weren't quick to forgive.

You may have been raised and schooled in a very forgiving environment, but cheating puts you in an entire different league. Once you're branded as a cheater, you lose credibility with not only the teacher whose classroom you cheated in, but with all your teachers. It's a mistake that keeps on hurting.

If you think of morality and credibility as easy to lose, and hard to gain back, you see how cheating can do some major damage. You do it once, and it doesn't seem like such a big deal the next time you do it, and even LESS of a deal the next time. If you're getting away with it, it only means you're depriving yourself of knowledge and study skills without anyone noticing. And if you don't get away with it, it's a blemish that's hard to rub off.

DR. LISA SAYS...

You might not care about what your teachers or the principal think. Pretty soon, you'll be out of that school, and their judgments won't matter. But your family will be with you forever. Do you want them to see you as the cheater in the family? Do you want them to always be questioning whether you really earned something or whether you cheated to get it? If you have younger siblings, think about what values you want to teach them. Do you want them to look up to you and be proud? Or to be held up to them as an example of what not to do?

> It was just a quiz, but after the teacher caught us, we all got Fs on the project. It was enough to bring my grade down one whole letter.

Definitely Not Good (You Hurt Your Reputation

PARENT SPEAK

Many kids state that low self-esteem contributed to their cheating at school. Here's something you can do: Find ways for your child to feel smart and competent in other parts of their life. If they're good at sports or music, incorporate something that lets them feel accomplished.

The more self-confident they feel, the less they'll feel the drive to win any way they can.

I f you are lucky enough to be getting away with your habit of cheating, you have to realize that luck runs out, and getting away with it once doesn't actually improve your chances of getting away with it next time. You may be an exceptional cheater, but do you really want to live in fear of the day that you cross paths with someone who can spot a cheater a mile away?

If you're caught cheating, it's one of those things that brands you for a long time afterwards.

> It takes many good deeds to build a good reputation, and only one bad one to lose it.
>
> —Benjamin Franklin

Schools are like villages; everyone's business seems to get around very quickly, and reputations are seemingly built up and ruined overnight. You don't want your friends to know you as a cheater, and you definitely don't want teachers or college admissions officers to see you as a cheater. Can you ever really prove to anyone that you won't do it again?

THE BASICS

reputation
n. the estimation in which a person or thing is held, esp. by the community or the public generally; repute: a man of good reputation. favorable repute; good name: to ruin one's reputation by misconduct.
a favorable and publicly recognized name or standing for merit, achievement, reliability, etc.: to build up a reputation.

Definition from dictionary.com

"Last year, I was all my teachers' favorite student. Then I got caught cheating and they all look at me like I smell bad or something."

Really, Really Bad (You Hurt Your Friends)

"Where did I go wrong?"

That's not a question you want your mother and father to be asking themselves, or saying aloud while they're sitting in the office of your school's principal receiving news of your bad behavior.

Perhaps in the past you haven't thought it through, but cheating shows a huge lack of respect. It shows disrespect to the parents who have devoted themselves to raising you right; it shows disrespect to your friends who are working hard for their grades; it shows disrespect to the school system that was set up to allow hard workers to get ahead.

If you've cheated, you were probably just trying to avoid work, or trying to get out of a desperate situation at the time. But you have no guarantee that the people around you won't interpret your action as having malicious intent.

That is not the impression you want to give to the people who care about you.

amily)

People that care about you want you to do well and if you're having trouble, they want to be there to help you. Instead of doing something, like cheating, that can potentially violate that trust and support, go to them first! Your friends will be able to listen to you talk about your problems, your parents can help you find some answers, and your teachers will help you gain the skills to overcome challenges on your own.

WHAT DO YOU DO?

In a moment of misjudgment, you agree to help your friend cheat on a test using a series of very subtle signals.

Right before the test however, you start to have misgiving, and tell your friend that you're not going to go through with it. He says, "you can't back out now." He threatens to tell your parents about this, and other plans you'd actually carried out in the past to help friends cheat.

"Children today are tyrants. They contradict their parents, gobble their food, and tyrannize their teachers."

—Socrates

Oh #@*%! (You Hurt Your Chances)

FOOD FOR THOUGHT

It was found in a study conducted at Arizona State University that half of all resumes for jobs reviewed contained false information, usually something big like a college degree, previous employment or a job title.

You now know that there's no surer way of screwing up your chances of getting into a good college than proving yourself a cheater. It's a hard lesson to learn, so the goal is to not learn it the hard way.

Cheating in school is one of the top reasons for denying a college application, according to a recent report. Students that cheat in school are considered unreliable and dangerous to the reputation of the college or university.

Some variation on how cheaters are tossed aside can be found well into adulthood in different parts of life. The most common and accepted reaction of girlfriends, boyfriends, and spouses to being cheated on by their significant other is to kick them to the curb. If you are found out to be lying on a job application, employers won't take a second look at the rest of your credentials, even if most of them were earned fairly.

The bottom line: if you get in the habit of cheating, there are many great opportunities you can miss out on. It is never worth it.

Cheating has both short and long term consequences, none of which are worth the short term gains of getting out of studying for a test or passing an exam you didn't think you could do well on by yourself.

THE BASICS

lie

n. a false statement made with deliberate intent to deceive; an intentional untruth; a falsehood: something intended or serving to convey a false impression.

> "There's so much pressure to get a good job, and to get a good job you have to get into a good school, and to get into a good school, you have to get good grades, and to get good grades you have to cheat."

Heck Yea! – Benefits of

> Sometimes the other kids make fun of us for not cheating and not passing crib notes. It's hard to take, but I wouldn't feel good about myself otherwise.

"Cheating is bad. We get it, we get it!"

Alright, The message is clear. Let's switch gears to a topic that's more uplifting, that we hope applies to a much higher number of you readers out there.

You've struggled, but made it. You've avoided temptation, taunts and tight deadlines and still managed to get through another school year

FOOD FOR THOUGHT

In a 2004 survey conducted by the Josephson Institute of Ethics, it was found that 98% of 25,000 students said it was important to them to be a person of good character. However, only 92% were satisfied with their ethics and character.

NOT Cheating

alive. You've kept your moral compass handy and we salute you. You should be proud of yourself.

You've avoided the pitfalls of cheating all this time. Maybe you slipped up once or twice, but you're trying hard not to do it again and you're doing alright at that so far. Need encouragement to keep up the good work? Well, there are plenty of benefits of not cheating that people in the position to cheat often overlook. Let's look at them!

> Though I am not naturally honest, I am so sometimes by chance.
>
> —William Shakespeare

THE BASICS

honesty

n. the quality or fact

of being honest;

uprightness and

fairness.

truthfulness, sincerity,

or frankness.

freedom from deceit

or fraud.

Nice! (You Can Hold Your Head Up High)

It is hard to do the right thing, especially when everyone else is doing the wrong thing, and happily. They may have their temporary rewards, but at the end of the day, you know you've got your honor, your discipline, and your morals intact. You're strong and proud, and you know it, even if you get the occasional B or C.

And don't think you're the only one who notices! Just as a bad reputation for cheating can follow you around, a good reputation for being an upstanding student can come in handy. If you

FOOD FOR THOUGHT

A 2000 study entitled "Report Card on the Ethics of American Youth" revealed that 78% of high school students have lied to their teachers.

Nothing builds self-esteem and self-confidence like accomplishment.

—Thomas Carlyle

ever find yourself in the unfortunate position of being wrongly accused of cheating, your clean record and your uncorrupted reputation among your peers speak for themselves.

But, as you already know, the benefits of not cheating exceed simply not getting fingered for something you didn't do. Accomplishing your goals through hard work and dedication helps to build vital self-esteem, something that will be the foundation for later, greater accomplishments.

F.Y.I.

Avoiding cheating in school will teach you the fundamentals of surviving in the real world. Uniqueness, focus, and creativity are all heavily rewarded in the work place. So if you avoid cheating now, you are setting yourself up for success in the future!

It feels good to accomplish things on my own, even though school is a tiring, busy, and sometimes frustrating place. Even so, I'm glad I'm doing it my way and not just copying someone else's work.

Sweet! (You Prove That You're Smart Enoug

DR. LISA SAYS...

Getting an A on a paper that someone else wrote does nothing for your own writing skills. When you put effort into studying and doing work on your own, you get genuine critiques from teachers that will really help you. You learn how to improve for the next time, which will make you smarter and more prepared for college and beyond. I always feel slightly guilty when I give a student a grade of 100% on a paper, since I'm not really doing my job and teaching that student something new.

I f you have resisted every single temptation to cheat, it's no doubt because you can see the big picture. You see beyond immediate benefits to the greater rewards and satisfactions in your future that can only be secured by not cheating.

"A" "B", "C", "D", or even a dreaded "F" grade is an insignificant speck in the entire scheme of your life; no single letter grade will ever make or

No student knows his subject: the most he knows is where and how to find out the things he does not know.

—President Woodrow Wilson

o Avoid a Common Pitfall)

break you, and you can see that. It's what you did or didn't do to earn that grade—your experience and how to build on it—that will serve you in life.

So while all the morons are wracking their brains to figure out how to illegitimately get those As they don't deserve, you're smarter than that, and be assured that though you'll have to give up some battles, you'll win the war.

FOOD FOR THOUGHT

Food, yes, food, can totally improve your ability to concentrate and do well in school. Try eating regularly and avoiding processed food and foods with chemical additives that mimic brain chemicals and slow you down. A balanced diet, full of colorful fruits and vegetables, will help you learn and work more efficiently.

> An excuse is worse than a lie, for an excuse is a lie, guarded.
>
> —Alexander Pope

Awesome! (You Learn Important Study Skills)

HALL OF SHAME

James Frey set the literary world ablaze with his startling memoir A Million Little Pieces, detailing his life as an alcoholic and drug abuser. He and his publisher claimed that the memoir was completely factual. This was revealed later to be untrue, as he had made up much of the dialogue and many of the events and characters. Frey lost the respect of the national reading community, and current editions of his book include a note by him apologizing for his fabrications. Frey had to withstand public criticism by the media, including a scathing verbal attack by Oprah Winfrey, who had previously trusted Frey enough to have had him as a guest on her show.

In some ways, a poor grade is more valuable to you than a good grade is. A grade that's not as good as you expected points out the areas in which you need improvement and prompts you to adjust your methods and study habits to do better next time. As hokey as that all sounds, this is how you grow, and how you learn to excel as a student. Edison didn't invent the light bulb the first time he tried -- in fact, most inventions took years of dedication.

In fact, it would be useful to look at your study skills from the point of view of a scientist. You experiment with your set of skills. You hone them, you build on them, you make them better, faster, stronger. It's a process, and cheating cheats you out of the crucial steps in the process. In an experiment, what good is an end result if you don't know how you got it? But we don't have to tell you... you already know this.

THE BASICS

accomplishment

1. n. an act or instance of carrying into effect; fulfillment: the accomplishment of our desires.
2. n. something done admirably or credit-ably: Space exploration is a major accomplishment of science.
3. n. anything accomplished; deed; achievement: a career measured in a series of small accomplishments.

"When you do nothing, you feel overwhelmed and powerless. But when you get involved, you feel the sense of hope and accomplishment that comes from knowing you are working to make things better."

—Unknown

Rock Out! (Knowing You Earned it All)

FOOD FOR THOUGHT

Believe it or not, exercise can clear your head and stimulate your brain, making studying more pleasant and effective. Don't like to exercise? Try taking a short walk. Twenty minutes a day has been shown to deliver results.

"It's the eye of the tiger,

It's the thrill of the fight,

Rising up to the challenge of our rival,"

If you've earned everything you've gotten, the band "Survivor" was singing about you, there. How does it feel to be the eye of the tiger?

"Because it's getting easier and easier to cheat these days, many kids have discarded the idea that hard work, study and thought are part of the educational experience. And then they're surprised when their non-cheating peers excel and they don't."

—Mr. Diaz, 12 grade chemistry teacher

Accomplishments are only sweet and satisfying when you know exactly how hard you worked to get them, and that's a fact. When you can dig back in your memory and track your progress, when you can see exactly how you succeeded, then you can feel real pride and you are ready for a repeat performance. Go ahead: look forward to a lifetime of piling your successes on top of each other. Know that they're all yours because you didn't cheat.

F.Y.I.

A report by the International Herald Tribune showed that people are prone to cheat even when it is not in their best interest. They suspend good judgment when they are faced with factors like peer pressure, self-image, and even their mood.

I've been asked what I do for tests if I don't cheat. What do they think? I'm up late every night with a book in my face until my Mom turns out the lights. Duh. I study.

Alternatives To Cheating

"Happiness is different from pleasure. Happiness has something to do with struggling, enduring, and accomplishing."

—Anonymous

T he alternative to cheating is not cheating. No surprise there.

But you probably need a better explanation than that if you are floundering in your schoolwork and feeling the pressure to get desperate.

You basically have the options of studying, memorizing, and practicing, and of finding different and more effective ways of doing each of these if one way isn't quite working for you. A common mistake however, is assuming that you are all alone in your struggles. There are entire industries set up to help students achieve their goals. You just have to find a solution that suits you.

F.Y.I.

27% of high school students, as reported by the "Report Card the Ethics of American Youth", said they'd lie to get a job.

It might take a while and a little trial and error to find what works best for you, but don't get discouraged along the way. Know that everyone learns differently and struggles at some point in their academic careers. It's also good to remember that everybody gets through it, one way or another. You just have to find what works best for you!

I would prefer even to fail with honor than to win by cheating.

—Sophocles

DR. LISA SAYS...

We hear a lot about "making the world a better place" by doing your part, no matter how small. Do you recycle in the hopes of stopping global warming? Donate a dollar for charity? Deciding to stop cheating can make a difference, too. Just like we all need to do our part to stop global warming and hunger, we all need to do our part to stop cheating, since it hurts us all. Do you really want your classmate to start operating on people after he cheated his way through medical school?

Hit the Books – Studying (Duh!)

PARENT SPEAK

Tutors aren't just for other kids. If your child is having trouble in a certain (or all) subject(s), get a tutor. They come in all shapes, sizes and price ranges. Be creative. But most importantly, get your student the help that he or she needs and deserves. It you want them to excel honestly, help students fight the good fight with the best weapons available.

There are the subjects that you are good at, and then there are the ones that really give you trouble.

What this usually means is that the study methods (and natural aptitudes) that work in some classes, don't work in others. If you find this is the case, or if you're not doing so hot in most of your classes, it's time to switch it up!

Experiment with different study methods. Take notes and highlight. Try using different colored

I'm relearning how to study and my friends and I have found some ways to make it fun. We get together for study groups and every Thursday we plan some sort of fun activity afterward. It's our reward for hard work and not only has the studying become easier, it's more fun too!

pens to keep things interesting as you do it. Make flashcards, turn off your TV or iPod and play soft classical music. Go to a library or coffee shop instead of working from home. Find the best way to hit those books, and hit them hard.

Also experiment with working at different times of day. Some students are so drained after school that an hour's worth of homework can only give 10 minutes worth of results. Try studying before school or right after lunch (don't forget to eat!) and take note of the times that your brain feels most receptive to learning.

And don't be afraid to keep trying and exercising different study skills until they work for you.

FOOD FOR THOUGHT

Your brain is a highly metabolic organ, which explains why you get hungry when you're thinking really hard for long periods of time.

Good "brain foods" include walnuts, raisins, fish, almonds, and yes, even some chocolate now and then doesn't hurt!

Hit them Up — Tutors, Study Group

Sometimes, try as you might, you just can't do it on your own. That's okay. Not every one is good at everything!

Tutors are great options for beefing up your learning methods and speed in any one subject. There are private tutors your parents can hire, and your school probably has set up volunteer tutoring programs for students who are serious about seeking out legitimate ways to get better grades (that's you!)

FOOD FOR THOUGHT

If you are having trouble studying for tests, try taking practice or sample tests as a method of studying. Maybe you could request your teachers to give you a few sample questions in order to help you understand their expectations. Also, textbook publishers often offer sample quizzes on their websites that pose as excellent tools for testing your knowledge.

"I'm studying better now and I've learned to ask my teachers for help. They're glad to answer questions. Before, I was always afraid they'd think I was stupid or something."

achers

If tutors are not an option, there are always study groups. This is where you can capitalize on the fact that you belong to a group of friends that you like and trust. If you organize study sessions, then get together and find ways to make them both helpful and fun (a nice plate of snacks for everyone, throw pillows on the carpet where everyone can spread out with their books), you might find that you've stumbled upon a way to make schoolwork enjoyable. Shocking!

And finally, you can always talk to your teachers. If you've tried your hardest and you're still struggling, sincerely letting a teacher know your concerns can nab you some sympathy points that will (honestly) get him or her to cut you some slack when grading your work. She or he will also be able to give you tips on what to focus on, what you're missing, etc. Demonstrating that you're interested in doing better, and doing what it takes to achieve more... that's admirable.

WHAT DO YOU DO?

Your parents have hired a college student who used to go to your high school as a private tutor to help you get through physics.

You're doing fine until you come to the chapter on gravity. You just can't seem to get it, despite the efforts of your tutor. One afternoon, she brings you an old test she's saved from when she took the test years ago.

"I know for a fact that that teacher is so lazy, there's no way he's changed the test since I took it."

What do you do?

Bottom Line: Cheating Suck

> "My best friend got caught texting the answers to her boyfriend for a geometry exam and was taken off our volleyball team, right before the championships. She was our best hitter and the whole team suffered because she couldn't play."

C heating sucks.

It sucks the fairness out of the school system.

It sucks the fun and satisfaction out of your accomplishments.

It sucks the chances for the future you're envisioning right out of your grasp.

HALL OF SHAME

In 2003, Lakers star Kobe Bryant was accused of rape by a young woman in Colorado. Though a judge later dismissed the charges against Kobe, the accusation and the fact that he had admittedly cheated on his wife tarnished his image.

He lost millions of dollars of endorsements, including contracts with McDonald's, Nutella, and Ferrero SpA.

It's never a good idea to start, and if you've started, the goal should be to stop and to find a way to regain all the things you've lost in the process, starting with your principles and your dignity.

If you've avoided cheating up 'til now, then congratulations are truly in order. You're on the right track and you're avoiding the traps so many of your peers have already fallen into.

Educators are trying to teach students to be free, critical thinkers. So where does cheating fit into that picture."

—Ms. Dalzell, 9th grade history

PARENT SPEAK

Make sure you and your child set reasonable expectations for their schoolwork. While all of us can always do better, make sure goals for improvement are incremental and attainable. And make sure your student can talk to you about his or her progress.

YOU'RE Better Than That... (Why You Do|

FOOD FOR THOUGHT

American psychologist Abraham Maslow described two kinds of esteem needs—the need for respect from others and the need for self-respect. Respect from others entails recognition, acceptance, status, and appreciation. Without the fulfillment of these needs, Maslow suggests, an individual feels discouraged, weak and inferior.

From Wikipedia.org

You don't need to cheat because you have pride in yourself and you have pride in your work. Even if it's not meeting the standards of any one teacher, your work is your own, and sooner or later you'll encounter a teacher who recognizes its merits.

You don't need to cheat because you're strong. You can withstand the pressure from your friends and classmates. You can withstand the pressure you're putting on yourself and can exercise logic even when panic is threatening to take over.

"Recently, I won an award for my piano performance. When I feel challenged at school and don't think I can do the work, I remember standing on that stage—and how happy I was—and it gives me new energy to tackle the task at hand."

eed To Do It)

You don't need to cheat because you're taking the long view and the high road. You see the person you want to be in the future, and you recognize that cheating will not let you become that person.

WHAT DO YOU DO?

Imagine yourself years from now, going up against a very intelligent Harvard graduate for a job at a successful company. It's your dream job, and you're pretty sure you've never wanted anything more in your entire life. After years of honest studying and hard work, you're very qualified for the job.

You also hear a rumor that your competitor's previous employers have suspected him of beefing up his resume with fake accomplishments. You have no way of proving that this is true, but you know your resume might not look as good in comparison now.

DR. LISA SAYS...

I work with some elementary school children, and here's what I say when I catch them cheating off each other: "Copy from him now, and you'll be copying from him later. Like when he's your boss, and you're re-peating what he orders you to do to make sure you got it right. Do it yourself, learn it, and you'll be the one giving the orders someday." It is hard to resist when others are cheating, but you have to look at it in a different way — you are learning, and they are not. So they may "win" in the short-term, but you'll come out ahead in the end.

...Even if THEY Aren't (How You Can Res

You don't need to cheat because you're smart. You can see through people, right down to their personal motivations for doing the dishonest things they do. They don't have control over themselves when they're cheating, so they won't have control over you!

Pressure comes from many external directions: school, your parents, your friends, your classmates. Sometimes it may seem unbearable. But taken one step at a time, you can manage the pressure and even make it work for you.

FOOD FOR THOUGHT

A survey by CollegeHumor.com had these findings to report: 12% of cheaters have been caught at some point in their cheating career. Only 7.1% of people who got caught stopped cheating after that.

"The pressure is overwhelming. There's pressure to get good grades, be popular, do well and not cheat. How do I handle all this pressure? Some days better than others."

ressure)

And now, you have a great advantage. You have a clear idea of all the unpleasantness that cheating can inflict on you in the near or distant future. You know exactly what you're avoiding when you don't cheat, and what you're gaining in the short and long term when you do things honestly.

You use all of these things you understand to resist cheating. When the "opportunity" to cheat comes around again, as it undoubtedly will, the choice will be easy for you.

THE BASICS

self-esteem
Synonyms or near-synonyms for self-esteem include:

self-worth
self-regard
self-respect
self-confidence
self-love

DR. LISA SAYS...

Cheating is kind of like taking steroids. When you're an athlete, it may seem like you need that edge to stay competitive, especially if you're surrounded by others who are also breaking the rules to get ahead. You may even get away with it for a while, but then, you just wind up permanently messing up your body, getting your records erased and losing your medals, rings, or trophies. Not too much endorsement money flowing in then, huh?

Ugh—Dealing With Failure

UGH—DEALING WITH FAILURE

" It was so unfair. One day all of us were hanging out before lunch and the next day they looked at me like I was the new kid. "

Y ou don't know what you've done, but it must be something. Do you smell bad? Did you say something? Maybe. Maybe not.

You know better than anyone how fickle other teens are. Today you're BFFs, tomorrow, you couldn't be any less.

Rejection is so hard to deal with and, because humans are thinking, feeling beings, it's hard not to analyze and overanalyze a rejection, especially one that you feel is undeserved. Teens, especially,

F.Y.I.

Rejection is something that happens to everyone, no matter how smart, attractive, talented or successful. Really.

PARENT SPEAK

are hard on themselves.

But before you let that guy or girl get to you and make you all depressed and gloomy, take a moment to look at the bright side. OK, there's no bright side, but it's not as bad as it seems right now. Tomorrow, they say, is another day.

How do you protect your child from life's rejections? You don't. But you can provide them with some tools for dealing with it. From friendships to dating, from sports to music, from teams to college admissions, your kid is going to be rejected. It's all part of life. But they don't always know that. Help your student avoid internalizing their pain by talking with them about rejection and sharing some of your life experiences. When they hear how you, and others, have managed rejection, it'll give them some tools to combat their own.

I take rejection as someone blowing a bugle in my ear to wake me up and get going, rather than retreat.

—Sylvester Stallone

Yeah, Yeah. Learning From Mistakes

Maybe your rejection isn't arbitrary, but is due to something you did or a problem you caused. But before you let one stupid mistake make you feel sad and self-conscious, ask yourself how to correct your mistake and, better yet, how not to repeat it.

Ask yourself what you did wrong and why are people mad at you. Be honest. It may be easy to gloss over your own bad behavior, but no one else will be. What would you do differently next time? If you hurt another person, can you apolo-

FOOD FOR THOUGHT

It's not always that bad. Sometimes you are going to say, or do, something inappropriate or offensive. Everyone has. Think about how many times your feelings have been hurt by some thoughtless words.

> Anyone who has never made a mistake has never tried anything new.
>
> —Albert Einstein

gize and try and make it right?

If your mistake is causing stresses that you don't know how to deal with, consider talking with a trusted teacher, counselor, parent, or family friend. Sometimes another person's perspective can really help.

Also, remember that time is a great healer. And sometimes there's nothing else to do but wait for the incident to blow over. It'll seem like forever, but it will blow over.

F.Y.I.

You know how everybody laughs when some guy comes out of the bathroom with toilet paper on his shoe, or when a snotty girl gets her dress stuck in her underwear? It's hideously embarrassing, but people get over it. No matter what you're feeling now, people *will* get over it.

" I was really mad because the other girls just stopped talking to me. It took a while before I realized that maybe it was my fault. "

Make A Plan: Getting Clear on What Yo

PARENT SPEAK

Helping your student recover from rejection or another failure can be one of the most valuable lessons you ever share. Validating their frustration can be just as important. Sure, you can tell them that life will get better, because it will. But if you're able to listen to their concerns and fears, and share some of your experiences, the exchange will have a great deal more value.

So here you are, staring down rejection again. Why did it happen another time? Could you have done something differently, or better?

The answer is all in the planning. Dissect the rejection. Was it social, academic, family- or work-related? Was it arbitrary or the result of under preparation or an overzealous wagging tongue?

Plan your comeback carefully. If you missed out on getting into a club or team because you didn't qualify, then the answer is easy: practice. If it's social, it may take a bit more thinking to figure out what went wrong and how/if you can correct it.

" Life is what happens to you while you're busy making other plans. "

——John Lennon

Vant

Think carefully and don't discount any reasonable solution—even if all seems hopeless. A few years ago, a high school senior applied to several universities and was accepted to three, but was wait listed at his first choice. His mother suggested he write a letter to the admissions board, thanking them for considering him and placing him on the wait list. How silly, he thought, but did it anyway. Two weeks later, he was admitted. Coincidence? Probably, but he'll never know.

"Don't spend your time beating yourself up over mistakes. Making mistakes is how you learn. Figure out how to do better the next time."

F.Y.I.

It might sound silly now, but eating right and getting enough sleep really do affect your moods and behavior. Try to eat some protein with your breakfast and make sure to stay hydrated so you can focus on school and not your growling stomach or parched throat.

Whoop, Whoop! The Victory Dance

Of course, most hard efforts don't end in failure. Most efforts reap glorious rewards. If you're working hard to overcome personal difficulties and start seeing the results, don't forget to celebrate!

As important as pushing yourself is congratulating yourself. When you know how to pat yourself on the back and allow yourself the perks of your success, you're creating your own motivation for keeping up the good work.

PARENT SPEAK

Noticing your student's successes is just as important as trying to help them through their failures. Tell your kids you're proud of them!

"The more you praise and celebrate your life, the more there is in life to celebrate."

—Oprah Winfrey

A date with the guy/girl you like? A spot on the prestigious choral group? Nice. A leisurely afternoon relaxing by the pool after the hard work is over and done with? Nicer.

Life is about balance, so work hard and play hard. Once you see the fruits of your labor, take the time to enjoy them. It will remind you what all the hard work is for and keep you motivated throughout your life.

F.Y.I.

The way to learn how to do something you want to do is to simply do it. Ask someone, take a class, practice. If you have the desire to do it, that's half the work.

> "Life has meaning only in the struggle. Triumph or defeat is in the hands of the Gods. So let us celebrate the struggle!"
>
> —Swami Sivandanda

Sailing On: Not Just Treading Water

FOOD FOR THOUGHT

According to the Mayo Clinic, people who practice positive thinking live longer and happier lives. Other benefits of being positive include:

✓ Decreased stress

✓ Greater resistance to catching the common cold

✓ A better sense of well-being

✓ Better overall health

✓ Improved coping skills

Maintaining a positive attitude is not only good for your physical and mental health, it's good for your grades, too. So is it possible to maintain a high level of positive thinking, and success, without resting too much on your laurels?

Simply put, yes. School can be very stressful and the academic and personal challenges rigorous. Maintaining a positive outlook, which celebrating achievements both small and great, better prepares you for long-term struggles.

"A man is but the product of his thoughts what he thinks, he becomes."

—Mahatma Gandhi

Do you sometimes look at other students who seem positive and wonder how they do it? While every person has their own attitude or technique, a good simple way to start is simply by languaging the attitude and behavior you want to exhibit. It may sound oversimplified, but merely by saying 'I will stay calm' or 'I am not going to let this test get the best of me' you are on your way to maintaining a calm and positive attitude.

Try it.

F.Y.I.

It might sound silly now, but eating right and getting enough sleep really do affect your moods and behavior. Try to eat some protein with your breakfast and make sure to stay hydrated so you can focus on school and not your growling stomach or parched throat.

"Everybody says 'think positive,' but sometimes the best I can do is try not to be negative."

Fighting Off What's Fighting
What Is It and How Can I Get Rid of It?

I'm so stressed," is something you've probably heard your friends say on almost a daily basis. Recently, you even find yourself chiming in with them when they complain about the mounds of homework they have or all their after school commitments. But what is stress really??

THE BASICS

stress

n. a specific response by the body to a stimulus, as fear or pain, that disturbs or interferes with the normal physiological equilibrium of an organism.

physical, mental, or emotional strain or tension: "Worry over his job and his wife's health put him under a great stress."

a situation, occurrence, or factor causing this: "The stress of being trapped in the elevator gave him a pounding headache."

ou: Stress Management

Stress is the way your body reacts to demands placed on it, whether that's your upcoming advanced Algebra exam or dealing with a difficult friend. When you feel stressed by something, your body releases chemicals into your bloodstream. These chemicals can have both positive and negative effects. Sometimes stress makes you work harder to get something done, but stress can also slow you down, especially if you have no way to deal with the extra energy the chemicals produce in you.

Here, we'll help you understand the causes of stress, signs of stress, how stress affects you, and the best ways to deal with it, because when you've already got so much to do, stress is the last thing you need to worry about.

> For fast-acting relief, try slowing down.
>
> ———Lily Tomlin

FOOD FOR THOUGHT

Many studies suggest that as students get to college, their sleeping schedule suffers greatly. Lack of sleep often results in the inability to concentrate, the need for more naps, and constant fatigue. Try getting a good rest and maybe this will give you more strength to deal with school and other issues.

Whadda Mean, Take a Deep Breath?

PARENT SPEAK

No one wants to believe that they've overlooked stress overload in their son or daughter. Here are a few signs to look for:

✓ high anxiety, which can lead to panic attacks

✓ feeling pressured, hassled, and hurried all the time

✓ mood swings and irritability

✓ physical symptoms: stomach problems, headaches, chest pain

✓ allergic reaction: eczema or asthma

✓ insomnia

✓ overeating, or worse, smoking or doing drugs

✓ depression

Stress affects everybody differently. Some people express themselves as angry or frustrated when stressed, while others can become withdrawn or depressed. None of these reactions are healthy and each can come with its own set of problems. People who take their aggressions out on people around them tend to alienate friends and loved ones while those who internalize stress can develop unhealthy ways of coping, such as eating disorders or substance abuse problems. As if you weren't stressed enough, already...

Believe it or not, stress is not always a bad thing, and it's very normal. It's your body's way of reacting to any change, whether it's positive or negative. And you've probably already figured out that stress is going to be with you throughout your school career—so the sooner you learn how to manage it, the better you'll be.

One of the first things people will tell you to do is 'take a deep breath.' What does that mean, really? Simply put: Stop for a moment. Sometimes you just need to step back and get some perspective on the situation for it to begin making sense. When we're stressed, our minds and bodies have a way of taking over, making it pretty hard to think straight. What can you do to 'take a breath' and get some perspective?

✎ Get up and walk away from the computer or desk.

✎ Go for a short walk (or do whatever exercise makes you feel better).

✎ Call a friend and talk about a lot of nothing for a while.

✎ Take a short nap.

✎ Listen to your favorite music.

FOOD FOR THOUGHT

A recent study revealed that over 60% of teenagers say that they watch more than 20 hours of television per week. The main reason? For relaxation.

How Can I Quiet My Mind with All Thes

FOOD FOR THOUGHT

Students who have learned to manage stress in their daily lives report that the following five items have helped them:

✓ Making a to-do list

✓ Setting realistic goals, both short- and long-term

✓ Stopping the cycle of worrying about "what if?"

✓ Avoiding over-scheduling

✓ Turning mistakes into lessons

When stress tightens its grip on you, it seems like there's no getting away. You may feel anxious, tired, frightened or angry and might not know how to deal with these emotions.

The truth is, everyone feels this way sometimes. It's not about the stress, it's about what you do with it. Sounds silly, right? But it's true.

The best way to deal with stress is not to avoid it, which is impossible, but to learn how to work with it. Here are a few suggestions for thinking about yourself and your well-being first:

✎ Try breathing exercises.

✎ Make an effort to think positively.

✎ Make time to relax and take a break.

✎ Read something uplifting or inspirational.

✎ Use positive visualization techniques—if you see it, you can do it!

✎ Talk it out with a friend or counselor.

ices?

🖎 Don't focus on the negative.

🖎 Take pride in your accomplishments.

🖎 Allow yourself to make some mistakes.

🖎 Eat something healthy.

🖎 Exercise.

🖎 Find something outside of school you like to do, and do it.

🖎 Make time for fun!

F.Y.I.

Use these four steps to problem solving:

1. Brainstorm solution
2. Think of the consequences
3. Choose a solution
4. Evaluate your choice

> "Don't underestimate the value of doing nothing, of just going along, listening to all the things you can't hear, and not bothering."
> —Pooh's Little Instruction Book, inspired by A.A. Milne

What Is It? Move or Sit Still?

D epending on your personality, different types of exercise may help you relieve stress. Yoga, which emphasizes quiet mediation, a focus on breathing, and lots of stretching and strengthening, can be great therapy for stress management.

FOOD FOR THOUGHT

A half an hour of exercise at least three times a week is an excellent way to get into shape and keep your body less tense. Start by walking around the neighborhood or maybe even enjoying a dance workout video!

"Part of being a winner is knowing when enough is enough. Sometimes you have to give up the fight and walk away, and move on to something that's more productive."

—Donald Trump

Yoga, is a non-competitive activity that gives everyone a chance to move at their own pace and focus on their own personal growth. With a competitive environment at school, yoga can give you the "breathing room" you need to deal with that stress.

Yoga is exercise that is good for the mind, body and soul and is an excellent outlet for those needing a little more quiet time in their lives. Sometimes when life is hectic, the best thing you can do is slow down and take some deep breaths.

F.Y.I.

Does Yoga seem too slow for you? Are you more into fast paced workouts? Try the new "hip" thing: Power Yoga. Power Yoga is essentially yoga with more swift and dynamic movements. It still gives your body that flexibility and ease, but also keeps you awake and refreshed!

" I never thought I had time for exercise until I started going with my roommate. Now I can't imagine not going. "

Exercise Does Calm the Body

For those who need to move around to burn off that extra energy, a high paced cardio workout might be a better solution. Something a simple as going for a run or jumping rope can allow you to focus again.

You don't have to go to the gym to get a good workout. You can take a run in your neighborhood or hike in the local park or foothills. When you're short on time, you can take a walk, get some fresh air, and burn a little stress energy.

FOOD FOR THOUGHT

Exercise is necessary for students because of the related cognitive benefits. What does that mean? When you move your body, your brain works better.
Enough said.

"There are thousands of causes for stress, and one antidote is to stress is self-expression. That's what happens to me. My thoughts get off my chest."

—Garson Kanin

Like a more structured routine? Sign up for an aerobic or spinning class or try kick boxing. Not only will you work out some aggressions, you'll build up some stamina, too.

Getting into a fitness routine doesn't have to be complicated—it's supposed to take your mind off stress. Enlisting a friend or workout buddy commits you to regular workouts and the time spent with someone you enjoy has added health benefits.

Try scheduling your exercise in with your other appointments. Not only will you be more inclined to show up and get moving, you'll avoid the guilt of missed workouts.

F.Y.I

According to recent studies, more than 70 million Americans walk to work out, making it the most popular form of exercise.

I'm really into my running workout. Running really helps me clear my head and makes me feel good, especially when I'm stressed.

—Katie Holmes

RESOURCES

Below are some great web resources for you and your parents to check out:

www.4Parents.org

www.AboveTheInfluence.com

www.TheCoolSpot.gov

www.DrDrew.com

www.Education.com

www.GirlsSpeakOut.org

www.IWannaKnow.org

www.Kaplan.com

www.KidsHealth.org

www.ParentingTeens.About.com

www.PreteenAlliance.org

www.ReachOut.com.au

www.TeenAdvice.About.com

THINGS TO THINK ABOUT

We've left you room to jot down notes of issues you want to discuss with friends, teachers or parents. We hope you use these pages as you read to personalize this book, and make it your own.

THINGS TO DO

THINGS TO DO

THINGS TO TALK TO MY TEACHERS/PARENTS ABOUT

THINGS TO TALK TO MY
TEACHERS/PARENTS ABOUT

THINGS TO TALK TO MY FRIENDS ABOUT

THINGS TO TALK TO MY FRIENDS ABOUT

JUST THINGS

JUST THINGS

JUST THINGS

Want more help dealing with the stress in your life? Look for these other books from Kaplan Publishing. Available wherever books are sold:

SOS Guide to Handling Peer Pressure
(Available in September 2008)

SOS Guide to Dealing with Tests
(Available in September 2008)

SOS Guide to Managing Your Time
(Available in March 2009)

SOS Guide to Getting Into Clubs and Sports
(Available in March 2009)

SOS Guide to Tackling Your Homework
(Available in March 2009)

Do your parents need a refresher course when it comes time to help you or your siblings with math homework? Tell them about:

Kaplan's Math for Moms and Dads
(Available October 2008)
This primer gives them all the terms, concepts, and helpful tips they've forgotten since high school.